Study in the Book of Daniel
Teaching Syllabus

Hilton Sutton, Th.D.

Institute of End Time Studies

(Daniel 5/10)

All Scripture quotations are taken from the *King James Version* of the Holy Bible.

Study in the Book of Daniel Teaching Syllabus
ISBN 978-1-4507-1508-9
Copyright © 2010
by Hilton Sutton
Institute of End Time Studies

www.hiltonsutton.org
1-800-367-9280

Dr. Hilton Sutton is one of the world's foremost authorities on the prophetic Scriptures, including the majestic book of Revelation. He is in great demand as a speaker for churches, Bible colleges, national and international conventions, and for radio and television audiences around the world. He teaches Bible prophecy without doom, gloom, or speculation in an edifying way that inspires victory, joy, peace, and hope, setting believers free from unscriptural fear of the future.

Following his military service during World War II, Dr. Sutton studied music at Lamar University. He attended the Southwestern Assemblies of God University upon accepting a call to the ministry. Centreville Bible College of the American Baptist bestowed a Doctorate of Divinity for his research, studies, and writing concerning the book of Revelation. Dr. Sutton's Doctorate of Theology is from Cornerstone University in Jerusalem, Israel. Also, an honorary Doctorate of Christian Ministries was bestowed in 1989 by El Seminario Teologico Misionero of Gautemala, C.A.

Presently, Dr. Sutton is president of Hilton Sutton World Ministries with executive offices in Allen, Texas. He is the leader and senior minister of Christ In You World Outreach, based in Uganda. He is a member of the Executive Board of World Ministry Fellowship of Plano, Texas, and was a founding trustee of the International Charismatic Bible Ministries of Tulsa, Oklahoma. He is also an active member of the International Convention of Faith Ministries of Arlington, Texas, and Faith Christian Fellowship of Tulsa, Oklahoma. He has personally addressed the Joint Chiefs of Staff of the United States Military, the Israeli Knesset and the Israeli Foreign Ministry. He is acquainted with Israeli Prime Minister Benjamin Netanyahu, and his personal friends include President Shimon Peres, Yitzak Shamir, the late Yitzak Rabin, and Menachem Begin.

Dr. Sutton has authored numerous books, including a verse-by-verse study of the book of Revelation entitled, *Revelation Revealed.* Its companion piece, *The Revelation Teaching Syllabus,* serves as a teaching guide to his fourteen-hour study of the book of Revelation available on CD and DVD. The Revelation study on DVD has been used for curriculum in many Bible schools, study groups, and churches around the world. *The Study in the Book of Daniel Teaching Syllabus* is a recent addition to Dr. Sutton's curriculum available through the Institute of End Time Studies. For more information about the Institute of End Time Studies, contact Hilton Sutton World Ministries.

Dr. Sutton's extraordinary collection of books, CDs and DVDs on the subject of Bible prophecy have blessed and edified hundreds of thousands of people in many nations. His sixty years of study and preaching the prophecies of the Scripture qualify him as the senior prophetic teacher of our day. Dr. Sutton's weekly telecast, *Bible Prophecy Unraveled,* is carried by the LeSea Television Network, World Harvest Television, and more than seventy stations including Direct TV and the AT&T Network.

For more information, please contact:

Hilton Sutton World Ministries

Phone: 1-800-367-9280

www.hiltonsutton.org
Email: hilton@hilton-sutton.org

Special Thanks!

As the apostle Paul was assisted by others during his ministry,

I have also been the recipient of the anointed talents of

family, staff and spiritual sons for which I am grateful.

Special thanks to Kevin Daisey for his dedication and research.

Kevin is a spiritual son to me as Timothy was to Paul.

His hours, days, weeks, months and years of study helped

create this Syllabus for which we are indebted.

— Hilton

Table of Contents

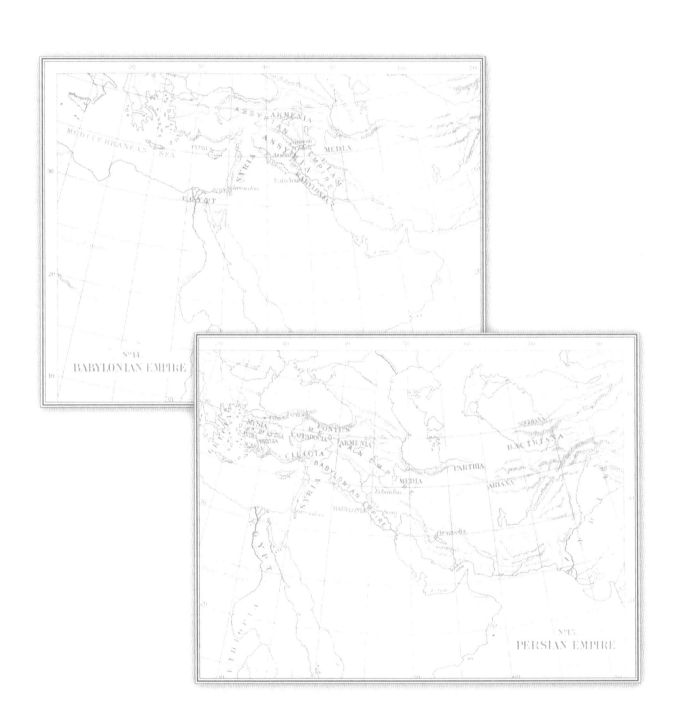

Nº 14.
BABYLONIAN EMPIRE

Nº 15.
PERSIAN EMPIRE

Introduction to
the Book of Daniel

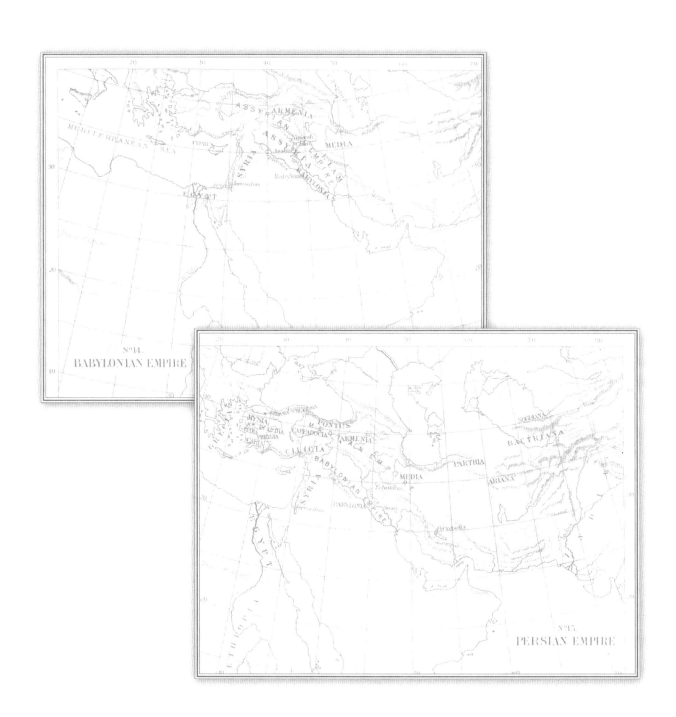

Nº 14.
BABYLONIAN EMPIRE

Nº 15.
PERSIAN EMPIRE

Introduction to the Book of Daniel

I. An Old Testament Overview.

1. Historical Books.

    A. The historical books include Genesis through Esther.

    B. The central theme of the historical books reflect the *Rise and Fall of the Hebrew Nation*.

    C. Genesis through Deuteronomy.

        (1) *Torah* is Hebrew for "law."

        (2) *Pentateuch* comes from the two Greek words "penta" (meaning "five") and "teuchos" (meaning "scrolls" or "books").

    D. First and Second Samuel (also referred to as the First and Second books of the Kings).

        (1) First Samuel describes the transition of leadership in Israel from judges to kings.

        (2) Samuel was the last judge of Israel who anoints their first king (Saul).

        (3) Second Samuel records major events of King David's forty-year reign, who lived at the halfway point between Abraham and Jesus Christ.

    E. First and Second Kings (also referred to as the Third and Fourth books of the Kings).

        (1) The first half of the book of First Kings traces the life of Solomon and Israel's rise to the peak of her size and glory.

        (2) In later years, pagan wives turn Solomon's heart away from God. This results in a king with a divided heart who leaves behind a divided kingdom.

        (3) The books of First and Second Kings then traces the twin histories of two sets of kings and two nations who have become indifferent to God's prophets and precepts.

    F. First and Second Chronicles.

        (1) Covers the same period of Jewish history found in Second Samuel through Second Kings.

        (2) The books of the Chronicles reflects this record with a spiritual flavor, while the books of First and Second Samuel, and First and Second Kings, are written with more of a historical flavor.

G. Ezra and Nehemiah.

    (1) Ezra continues the history of Second Chronicles revealing God's promise to restore the Jewish people to their homeland after being in captivity for seventy years.

    (2) Zerubbabel rebuilds the temple (this is their first return from Persia).

    (3) Ezra rebuilds the spiritual condition of the people (this is their second return from Persia).

    (4) Nehemiah, a contemporary of Ezra, leads the third and final return of the Hebrew people back to Jerusalem after their captivity in Babylon. The purpose of this return is to rebuild the walls and the city.

H. Esther.

    (1) The book of Esther dovetails between the sixth and seventh chapters of Ezra. Esther falls between the first and second returns to Jerusalem from Persia, led by Zerubbabel and Ezra, respectively.

    (2) Esther is the only biblical record of the vast majority of Jewish people who remained in Persia rather than return for the rebuilding in Jerusalem.

2. Poetic Books.

A. The poetic books include Job through Solomon.

B. The central theme of the poetic books reflects the *Golden Age of Israel*.

Notes: _____

_____

_____

_____

_____

_____

_____

_____

_____

_____

_____

_____

_____

_____

_____

_____

_____

_____

3. Prophetic Books.

    A. The prophetic books include Isaiah through Malachi.

    B. The writings within the prophetic books cover a period of approximately 400 years (Obadiah 840 B.C. – Malachi 425 B.C.).

    C. Seventeen prophetic books were authored by sixteen prophets (Jeremiah also authored the book of Lamentations).

    D. Four Major Prophets.

        (1) Isaiah   (3) Ezekiel

        (2) Jeremiah   (4) Daniel

    E. Twelve Minor Prophets.

(1) Hosea	(5) Jonah	(9) Zephaniah
(2) Joel	(6) Micah	(10) Haggai
(3) Amos	(7) Nahum	(11) Zechariah
(4) Obadiah	(8) Habakkuk	(12) Malachi

    F. Thirteen prophets identify with the destruction of Israel.

(1) Isaiah	(6) Joel	(10) Micah
(2) Jeremiah	(7) Amos	(11) Nahum
(3) Ezekiel	(8) Obadiah	(12) Habakkuk
(4) Daniel	(9) Jonah	(13) Zechariah
(5) Hosea		

    G. Three prophets identify with the restoration of Israel under the Persian Empire. The restoration was accomplished under the leadership of Zerubbabel, Ezra and Nehemiah.

        (1) Haggai   (2) Zechariah   (3) Malachi

Notes: _____

_____

_____

_____

_____

_____

_____

_____

_____

_____

_____

Study in the Book of Daniel

II. Four Prophetic Keys.

1. Major Theme and Prediction of the Prophets.

   The God of Israel would become the God of all nations.

2. Mission of the Prophets.

   Saving Israel from idolatry and wickedness.

3. Message of the Prophets.

   The destruction of Israel would come, and a remnant of Israel would be saved. From that remnant, the "branch" would come from the bloodline of David who would turn all nations back to God.

4. Single Most Important Event of the Old Testament Prophets.

   The destruction of the city of Jerusalem.

Notes: _____

_____

_____

_____

_____

_____

_____

_____

_____

_____

_____

_____

_____

_____

_____

_____

_____

_____

_____

_____

_____

_____

_____

_____

III. The Divided Kingdom.

1. The downfall of the Hebrew Nation began when the people rejected God as their King, demanding a natural king in order to be like all of the nations (I Samuel 8).

2. The twelve tribes of Israel divided in approximately 931 B.C.

3. The division of the Hebrew Nation is described in First Kings 11:1-13. God's warning in verses 9-13 came as a result of Solomon turning his heart toward the gods of his pagan wives and concubines (1,000 in all), worshiping the following gods:

   A. Ashtoreth – goddess of sensual love.

   B. Molech – required the sacrifice of children by fire.

   C. Milcom – associated with the god Molech.

   D. Chemosh – required the sacrifice of children by fire (built an altar on the Mount of Olives).

4. Biblical and historical record reflects the fact that the nation of Judah would occupy the land made up of one tribe for David (Judah), and one tribe for Jerusalem's sake (Benjamin). That land would be given to Solomon's son, Rehoboam (I Kings 11:13).

5. Ten tribes revolt and occupy the northern territory known as *Israel* (931 B.C.). The remaining tribes (Judah and Benjamin), located to the south made up the territory of *Judah*. (See II Chronicles 10; 11:1-12; I Kings 12.)

IV. The Destruction of the Hebrew Nation.

1. The fall of the Hebrew Nation (Israel and Judah), came about in two separate events.

2. The Northern Kingdom of Israel fell first to the Assyrian Empire between the approximate years of 721-713 B.C.

3. Around that same period, the following prophets had, or were in the process of ministering:

Israel

A. Amos (760-753 B.C.)

B. Hosea (760-720 B.C.)

Judah

A. Joel (830-750 B.C.)

B. Isaiah (740-680 B.C.)

C. Micah (735-710 B.C.)

Nineveh

(Assyrian capital)

A. Jonah (782-753 B.C.)

Edom

(Descendants of Esau)

A. Obadiah (840 B.C.)

4. The destruction of Judah came about 100 years later after Israel fell to the Assyrian Empire.

5. The Southern Kingdom of Judah was destroyed by the Babylonian Empire under King Nebuchadnezzar beginning between the years of approximately 608-605 B.C., and again in 597 B.C. The city of Jerusalem was burned in 586 B.C.

6. Around that time period, the following prophets had, or were in the process of ministering:

Judah

A. Zephaniah (640-609 B.C.)

B. Jeremiah (626-586 B.C.)

C. Habakkuk (606 B.C.)

Babylon

A. Daniel (605-530 B.C. in the king's court)

B. Ezekiel (593-571 B.C. in captivity)

Nineveh

(Assyrian capital)

A. Nahum (663-612 B.C.)

V.   The Restoration of the City of Jerusalem.

1. Under the Persian Empire, Judah was permitted to rebuild the temple and the city of Jerusalem. The rebuilding took place under the leadership of Zerubbabel, Ezra and Nehemiah beginning in approximately 539-536 B.C.

2. During this period of restoration in Jerusalem, the following prophets were ministering:

Jerusalem

A. Haggai (520 B.C.)

B. Zechariah (520 B.C.)

C. Malachi (432-425 B.C.)

3. Zerubbabel's first return was to rebuild the temple in 536 B.C. (under the decree of King Cyrus of Persia given in 539 B.C.). A portion of the Jewish population (49,897) returned to Jerusalem under his leadership (Ezra 2:64-65).

4. The rebuilding of the temple was discontinued around 534 B.C., resumed in 520 B.C., and was completed in 515 B.C. It began under King Cyrus and finished under King Darius I.

5. The prophets Haggai and Zechariah ministered in Jerusalem during Zerubbabel's restoration.

6. The historical book of Esther dovetails between the first return of Zerubbabel and the second return under Ezra (between Ezra chapters 6 and 7). Esther is the only biblical account of the Jewish population that remained in Persia while 49,897 returned to Jerusalem. Esther is the stepmother of King Artaxerxes I (Esther 2:15-18) who deposed Queen Vashti (mother of King Artaxerxes I), becoming the queen of Persia. Later, King Artaxerxes I decrees the return of Nehemiah to rebuild Jerusalem.

7. Ezra leads the second return of 1,754 (Ezra 8:1-20) to Jerusalem in 457 B.C., under the decree of King Artaxerxes I of Persia (Ezra 7:11-26). Their return came seventy-nine years after Zerubbabel's ministry in 536 B.C. (Ezra 1 and 2). Ezra went to restore the people both spiritually and morally.

8. Nehemiah serves as the cupbearer to King Artaxerxes I of Persia who decrees a request of Nehemiah to rebuild the *"city of my father's sepulchers"* (Nehemiah 2:1-8). This decree went forth on March 4, 444 B.C. This third return from Persia to Jerusalem was thirteen years after Ezra's second return in 457 B.C., and ninety-two years after Zerubbabel's ministry in 536 B.C.

9. The walls were completed under Nehemiah's leadership in fifty-two days (Nehemiah 6:15). Malachi prophesied from 432-425 B.C. Nehemiah took 150 skilled men to Jerusalem.

10. The decree of King Artaxerxes I (Nehemiah 2:1-8) on March 4, 444 B.C. establishes the prophetic dateline for Daniel's "seventy weeks" prophesied by Daniel (Daniel 9:24-27), in approximately 538 B.C.

11. During the period covered by Zerubbabel, Ezra and Nehemiah (approximately 539-425 B.C.), the following false prophets were on the scene:

    A. Buddha (560-480 B.C.) in India.

    B. Confucius (551-479 B.C.) in China.

    C. Socrates (470-399 B.C.) in Greece.

Notes: _____

_____

_____

_____

_____

_____

_____

_____

_____

_____

Study in the Book of Daniel

VI. The Priesthood Ministry.

1. The ministry of the priesthood is hereditary from the tribe of Levi.

2. The priesthood was made up of appointed religious teachers.

VII. The Prophetic Ministry.

The prophets and their position, unlike the priesthood, is not inherited but called of God. The prophets came from various backgrounds:

1. Jeremiah   – Priesthood

2. Ezekiel   – Priesthood

3. Zechariah   – Priesthood

4. Isaiah   – Royal Blood

5. Daniel   – Royal Blood

6. Zephaniah – Royal Blood

7. Amos   – Shepherd

VIII. The Central Theme of the Prophets.

1. Major Prophets
   A. Isaiah   – *God has a remnant and it has a glorious future.*
   B. Jeremiah   – *Jerusalem's sin, destruction, and its future glory.*
   C. Ezekiel   – *Fall of Jerusalem, its restoration, and glorious future.*
   D. Daniel   – *Four Kingdoms (Babylon, Persia, Greece, Rome); and God's Everlasting Kingdom.*

Notes: _____

_____

_____

_____

_____

_____

_____

_____

_____

_____

_____

_____

_____

2. Minor Prophets

    A.   Hosea   –   *Jehovah will become the God of all nations.*

    B.   Joel   –   *A vision of the Gospel Age and the ingathering of all nations.*

    C.   Amos   –   *The House of David will yet rule the world.*

    D. Obadiah   –   *Edom (the descendants of Esau) will be destroyed.*

    E.   Jonah   –   *God is interested in His enemies (of Israel).*

    F.   Micah   –   *Coming Prince of Bethlehem and His universal reign.*

    G. Nahum   –   *Judgment for Nineveh (the capital city of the Assyrians).*

    H. Habakkuk –   *Triumph for God's people.*

    I.   Zephaniah –   *There will come a new revelation and God's people will be called by a new name.*

    J.   Haggai   –   *The second temple (under the Persian Empire) and the coming greater temple.*

    K. Zechariah –   *The coming King; His house and kingdom.*

    L.   Malachi   –   *The closing message of the Messianic nation.*

IX.   The Order of the Prophets.

Canonical Order	Chronological Order	Chronological Date
1. Isaiah	Obadiah	840 B.C.
2. Jeremiah	Joel	830 B.C.
3. Ezekiel	Jonah	782 B.C.
4. Daniel	Amos	760 B.C.
5. Hosea	Hosea	760 B.C.
6. Joel	Isaiah	740 B.C.
7. Amos	Micah	735 B.C.
8. Obadiah	Nahum	663 B.C.
9. Jonah	Zephaniah	640 B.C.
10. Micah	Daniel	605 B.C.
11. Nahum	Jeremiah	626 B.C.
12. Habakkuk	Habakkuk	606 B.C.
13. Zephaniah	Ezekiel	593 B.C.
14. Haggai	Haggai	520 B.C.
15. Zechariah	Zechariah	520 B.C.
16. Malachi	Malachi	432 B.C.

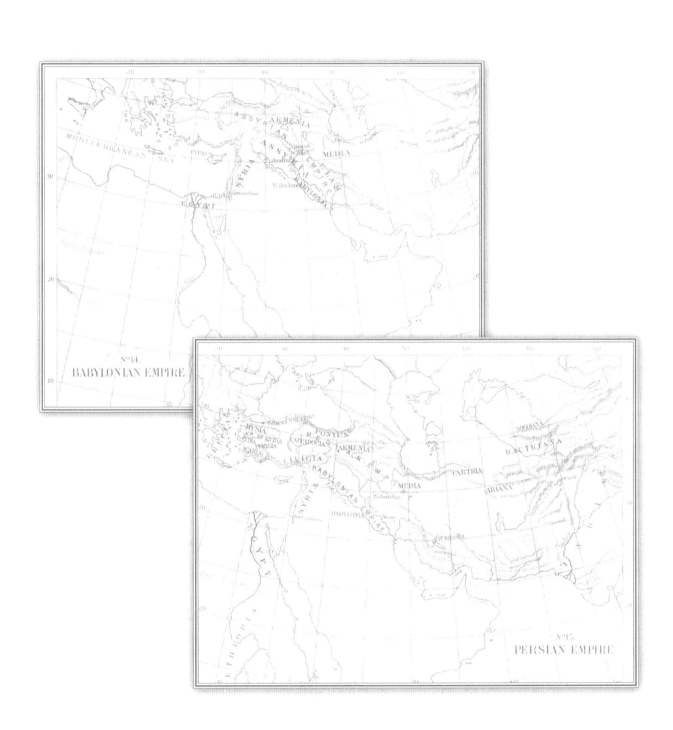

The Prophet Daniel

The Prophet Daniel

I. Prophetic Ministry Overview.

1. The central theme of Daniel is *Four Kingdoms (Babylon, Persia, Greece and Rome); and God's Everlasting Kingdom.*

2. The prophet Daniel was apparently of royal blood, being born to a noble Judean family (Daniel 1:3-4).

3. Daniel was taken into Babylonian captivity during the first of three sieges against Judea and Jerusalem, conducted by Nebuchadnezzar in approximately 605 B.C.

4. Daniel was approximately seventeen years of age (born 622 B.C.). Ezekiel was approximately eighteen years of age at that time. The prophet Jeremiah was approximately twenty years their senior. Ezekiel went into captivity during the second siege of the city of Jerusalem in 597 B.C. (Ezekiel and Daniel were approximately twenty-six and twenty-five years of age respectively at that time).

5. Eleven years later, the city of Jerusalem was captured and burned in 586 B.C.

6. Daniel served in the king's court of:
   A. Nebuchadnezzar in Babylon.
   B. Cyrus and Darius in Persia.[1]

7. The contemporaries of Daniel.[2]
   A. Ezekiel (Babylon captivity – 593-571 B.C.).
   B. Habakkuk (Judah – 606 B.C.).
   C. Zephaniah (Judah – 640-609 B.C.).
   D. Nahum (Nineveh – 663-612 B.C.).

---

[1] Zerubbabel's first return to rebuild the temple in Jerusalem occurred in 536 B.C. under King Cyrus of Persia. Babylonian captivity endured from 605 until 536 B.C. (seventy years).

[2] Jesus supports the writings of Daniel in Matthew 24:15. Ezekiel supports Daniel in Ezekiel 14:14.

Notes: _____

_____

_____

_____

_____

Study in the Book of Daniel

II. Daniel's Major Prophetic Teachings.

1. Daniel chapter 1.

   A. Daniel is carried into Babylonian captivity in 605 B.C. at the approximate age of seventeen.

   B. Daniel (Belteshazzar), Hananiah (Shadrach), Mishael (Meschach) and Azariah (Abednego) were taken into captivity. All were of royal blood in Judah. All were given new names.

   C. Daniel continued in the king's court and found favor there.

2. Daniel chapter 2.

   A. Nebuchadnezzar dreams of a "terrible image" (verse 31).

   B. Daniel interprets Nebuchadnezzar's dream (verses 36-45).

   C. Daniel describes the "terrible image" as four earthly kingdoms:

      (1) Golden Head – Babylon

      (2) Silver Chest and Arms – Persia (Media)

      (3) Thighs of Brass – Greece

      (4) Legs of Iron, Feet of Iron and Clay – Rome

   D. Daniel describes four empires, some under which he lived.

      (1) Daniel describes the "golden head" as *Babylon*, the empire under which he was taken captive.

      (2) Daniel describes the "arms of silver" as *Persia*. The two arms of silver identifies the two groups that made up Persia, namely the Persians and the Medes.

      (3) Daniel describes *Greece* as the "thighs of brass." Alexander the Great conquered Egypt and the Persian Empire in the Middle East, along with Macedonia in Europe. He built the Greek Empire by uniting the east and the west.

Notes: _____

_____

_____

_____

_____

_____

_____

_____

_____

(4) Daniel describes the *Empire of Rome*:

    a. First as two "legs of iron." The two feet and ten toes were made of "iron and clay."

    b. The Roman Empire divided in A.D. 364. The Western Division was the (Papal Church) and the Eastern Division was the (Greek Church). The two legs of Daniel's "terrible image" represented the Eastern and Western divisions of Rome.

    c. *"This image . . . his legs of iron, his feet part of iron and part of clay"* (Daniel 2:31-33).

    d. *"And the fourth kingdom [Rome] shall be strong as iron: forasmuch as iron breaketh in pieces and subdueth all things: and as iron that breaketh all these, shall it break in pieces and bruise. And whereas thou sawest the feet and toes, part of potter's clay, and part of iron . . . so the kingdom [Rome] shall be partly strong, and partly broken"* (Daniel 2:40-42).

    e. *"Then I would know the truth of the fourth beast [Rome], which was diverse from all the others, exceeding dreadful, whose teeth were of iron, and his nails of brass; which devoured, brake in pieces, and stamped the residue with his feet; and of the ten horns that were in his head, and of the other which came up, and before whom three fell; even of that horn that had eyes, and a mouth that spake very great things . . ."* (Daniel 7:19-20).

    f. *"I saw in the night visions, and behold a fourth beast [Rome], dreadful and terrible, and strong exceedingly; and it had great iron teeth: it devoured and brake in pieces . . . and it had ten horns"* (Daniel 7:7).

    g. *"I considered the horns, and, behold there came up among them another little horn, before whom there were three of the first horns plucked up by the roots: and, behold, in this horn were eyes like the eyes of a man, and a mouth speaking great things"* (Daniel 7:8).

Notes: _____

_____

_____

_____

_____

_____

_____

_____

_____

_____

_____

Study in the Book of Daniel

h. Turmoil exists stemming from three kingdoms that produce the Antichrist. Those three kingdoms are removed from that system.

i. *"The fourth beast shall be the fourth kingdom upon earth* [Rome] *... and the ten horns out of this kingdom* [Rome] *are ten kings that shall arise: and another* [the Antichrist] *shall rise after them; and he* [the Antichrist] *shall be diverse from the first, and he* [the Antichrist] *shall subdue three kings"* (Daniel 7:23-24).

j. *"And there appeared another wonder in heaven; and behold a great red dragon, having seven heads and ten horns, and seven crowns upon his heads"* (Revelation 12:3).[3]

k. *"I will tell thee the mystery of the woman, and the beast that carrieth her, which hath the seven heads and ten horns"* (Revelation 17:7).

l. *"And here is the mind which hath wisdom. The seven heads are seven mountains* [seven kingdoms] *... and there are seven kings* [over seven kingdoms]: *five* [kingdoms] *are fallen* [Egypt, Assyria, Babylon, Persia, Greece], *and one* [kingdom] *is* [Rome], *and the other is not yet come* [the kingdom that produces the Antichrist]; *and when he* [the Antichrist] *cometh, he must continue a short space"* (Revelation 17:9-10).

m. The first five kingdoms that *"are fallen"*:

(i) Egyptian Empire – **first head**

(ii) Assyrian Empire – **second head**

(iii) Babylonian Empire – **third head**

(iv) Persian Empire – **fourth head**

(v) Greek Empire – **fifth head**

n. The *"one"* kingdom that *"is"*:

(i) Roman Empire – **sixth head**

o. The kingdom that *"is not yet come"*:

(i) The kingdom that produces the Antichrist – **seventh head**

---

[3] Revelation 12:9 identifies the *"dragon"* as Satan, the Devil.

E. Daniel's Kingdom that births the Antichrist.

  (1) The Antichrist comes up out of Daniel's *"fourth beast"* (Daniel 7:7-8), which identifies Daniel's fourth kingdom, *Rome* (Daniel 7:17).

  (2) Out of Daniel's fourth beast, or fourth kingdom (the Roman Empire):

    a. Shall arise ten kings (Daniel 7:7, 24).

    b. Ten toes (Daniel 2:40-43).

    c. Ten horns/ten kings (Revelation 17:11-12). Refers to the present European Union.

F. The Kingdom of the Antichrist - **eighth head**.

  (1) The Antichrist (eighth head) shall arise from a ten nation confederation of kingdoms (seventh head) that shall originate from the geographic area of the Roman Empire, modern day Europe (sixth head) (Revelation 17:11).[4]

  (2) The following treaties were signed in Rome on March 25, 1957:

    a. European Atomic Energy Community (Euratom).

    b. European Economic Community (EEC); the "Common Market."

    c. These two treaties became known as the "Treaties of Rome."

G. Identical Parallel Kingdom(s) and Bible References.[5]

Daniel 7	Revelation 13
(1) (verse 4) Lion	(verse 2) Lion
(2) (verse 5) Bear	(verse 2) Bear
(3) (verse 6) Leopard	(verse 2) Leopard
(4) (verse 7) Beast with Iron Teeth	

---

[4] These ten nations will receive power as kings with the Beast for a short time. They shall give their power and strength to the Beast. These shall make *"war with the Lamb,"* and shall be overcome at the Battle of Armageddon (Revelation 17:12-14), along with the 200 million-man Oriental army (Revelation 9:14-16; 16:12,16).

[5] The ten horns of the seventh head of the Beast in Revelation chapters 13 and 17 correspond with the ten horns of Daniel chapter 7.

Notes: _____

_____

_____

_____

_____

_____

H) The Deadly Wounded Empire.

   (1) Revelation 13:3 describes one of the seven heads, *"And I saw one of his heads as it were wounded to death."*

   (2) Each "head" is identified by Daniel as a world empire.

   (3) Daniel 2:34 describes his fourth kingdom (Rome) by saying it was *"Smote . . . upon his feet"* by the *"stone cut out without hands"* that *"filled the whole earth"* (Daniel 2:34-35).

   (4) Jesus was born on earth during the Roman Empire (sixth head). Jesus is described as the *"Rock"* in I Corinthians 10:4. Matthew 24:14 declares that the *"gospel of the kingdom shall be preached in all the world for a witness unto all nations; and then shall the end come."*

   (5) The Roman Empire was the "head" given the death blow by Jesus. The same "head" is resurrected as modern day Europe under the Treaties of Rome, or the European Economic Community (the Common Market) signed in Rome on March 25, 1957.

3. Daniel chapter 3.

   A. The fiery furnace account with:

      (1) Hananiah (Shadrach).

      (2) Mishael (Meschach).

      (3) Azariah (Abednego).

4. Daniel chapter 4.

   A. Nebuchadnezzar has a second dream. He spends seven years in the wilderness as a wild man until he returns to honor God.

   B. God's grace dealt with Nebuchadnezzar for twelve months before he experiences those seven years in the wilderness (verse 29).

   C. Nebuchadnezzar recognizes the God of heaven and accepts Him. The king becomes numbered among the righteous.

Notes: _____

_____

_____

_____

_____

_____

_____

_____

_____

5. Daniel chapter 5.

   A. Belshazzar becomes the new king of Babylon at the age of thirty.

   B. Belshazzar holds a celebration for 1,000 people, while calling for the use of the vessels that were taken from the temple in Jerusalem by his grandfather, King Nebuchadnezzar.

   C. Daniel is called to interpret the writings that appear on the wall of the hall during that feast.

   D. Daniel's interpretation reveals that the kingdom of Belshazzar is finished.

   E. The kingdom of Babylon was given over into the hands of Darius at the approximate age of sixty-two.

6. Daniel chapter 6.

   A. Daniel is made the first president over the Persian Empire by Darius the king of Persia (verses 1-2).

   B. Darius the king is deceived by 120 princes and two other presidents (verses 4-9) to sign a law to prohibit prayer in the Persian Empire to anyone except himself.

   C. Daniel is sent to the lion's den. His life is spared.

   D. Those accusers of Daniel are executed in the lion's den (verse 24).

7. Daniel chapter 7.

   A. Daniel has a vision of four great beasts:

      (1) Lion   – Babylon

      (2) Bear   – Persia

      (3) Leopard   – Greece

      (4) Iron tooth beast – Rome

   B. The four beasts represent four kings and four kingdoms (verse 17). (See Revelation chapters 13:1-2 and 17:7-12.)

   C. The ten horn Beast System and the Antichrist is described (verse 8).

   D. Christ foretold (verses 13-14).

   E. The power and dominion stripped from the Antichrist (verses 18, 26-27).

Notes: _____

_____

_____

_____

_____

_____

8. Daniel chapter 8.

   A. Persia is symbolized by a *"ram"* (verse 20).

   B. The ram had *"two horns"* (verses 3, 20), the last horn rose higher than the first horn.

      (1) The Persian Empire was made up of two powers:

         a. Media

         b. Persia

      (2) Persia and Media were united under Cyrus the Great in 550 B.C., followed by King Darius as they built a united empire.

      (3) Persia expanded its territory by conquering Babylon to the northwest in 539 B.C. and Egypt to the southwest in 525 B.C. (verse 4).

   C. Greece is symbolized by a *"goat"* (verse 21).

      (1) The goat has one *"horn"* between his eyes (verse 5).

      (2) That horn represents the first king of Greece (verse 21).

      (3) Alexander the Great conquered Persia between 334 and 323 B.C. Alexander died later that year.

      (4) Four generals followed after Alexander the Great:

         a. General Cassandar – Greece and Macedonia

         b. General Lysimachus – Asia Minor (Turkey)

         c. General Seleucus – all Eastern parts of the Greek Empire including Syria, Iraq and Iran.

         d. General Ptolemy – Egypt, Palestine, Arabia.

Notes: _____

_____

_____

_____

_____

_____

_____

_____

_____

_____

_____

_____

_____

_____

(5) Antichrist identified (verses 23-25):

    a. He is of *"fierce countenance."*

    b. He has *"understanding dark sentences."*

    c. He is a destroyer.

    d. His *"power shall be mighty, but not by his own power"* (see also Revelation 13:2),

    e. He uses witchcraft,

    f. He *"shall magnify himself in his own heart."*

    g. He *"shall stand up against the Prince of princes; but he shall broken."* This occurs at Armageddon (Revelation 19).

9. Daniel chapter 9.

    A. The prophetic timeline of the "seventy weeks" of Daniel set forth (verses 24-27).

      (1) *"Seventy weeks are determined upon thy people."*

      (2) According to Daniel 1:6, Daniel's people are the descendants of Israel from the tribe of Judah.

      (3) Therefore all of the 490 years are directed toward the descendants of Israel, not the Church.

      (4) Daniel's *"seventy weeks"* begin with *"the going forth of the commandment to restore and to build Jerusalem"* (verse 25).

      (5) That decree for rebuilding the city was given by King Artaxerxes I of Persia to Nehemiah (Nehemiah 2:1-8). History records this event occurring on March 4, 444 B.C.

      (6) The "sixty-nine weeks" pinpoints the coming of the Messiah. Sixty-nine weeks equals 483 years.

Notes: _____

_____

_____

_____

_____

_____

_____

_____

_____

(7) Forty-nine years (seven weeks) are required for the rebuilding of the "street and wall, even in troublous times" (verse 25). Sixty-two weeks (434 years), would elapse once the city was rebuilt until Jesus would enter Jerusalem and be crucified or *"cut off"* (verse 26).

(8) Verse 27 provides insight into the 70th and final week that is to be accounted for and *"determined upon thy people"* (see Daniel 1:6), known as "the Tribulation."

B. The Tribulation.

(1) Daniel 9:27 shows that the Tribulation is seven years long and is divided into two equal halves of 3 1/2 years each.

(2) Revelation 11:2-3 describes the last half of the Tribulation Period of forty-two months (1260 days), or 3 1/2 prophetic years (thirty days per month and 360 days per year).

(3) Daniel 9:27 depicts the "Time of the Antichrist" as a seven-year period that corresponds to the Tribulation. The beginning of the Antichrist's earthly operation is consistent with the release and deception of the rider of the white horse found in Revelation 6:2.

(4) Second Thessalonians 2:3-9 provides additional insight to the "Time of the Antichrist" as *"that man of sin . . . might be revealed in his time."*

(5) Daniel 9:27 reveals the Antichrist will enter into an agreement, or *"covenant,"* with Daniel's people at the onset of that seven-year Tribulation Period.

(6) Daniel 8:25 defines that covenant as one that will include a policy of peace. This peace will be the means by which the Antichrist *"shall destroy many."*

(7) The *"peace"* that *"shall destroy many"* results in a world war that is described in Ezekiel 38 and 39. It is further confirmed by the rider of the red horse at the onset of the Tribulation (Revelation 6:3-4).

(8) The ministry of the 144,000 begins at the conclusion of this world war as described in Ezekiel 9, Zechariah 8:23 and Revelation 7:1-8; 14:1-4.

Notes: _____

_____

_____

_____

_____

_____

C. Mid-Tribulation.

    (1) Daniel 9:27 denotes the breaking of the covenant *"in the midst of the week,"* or 3 ¹/₂ years into the Tribulation.

    (2) Second Thessalonians 2:4 further describes the plans of the Antichrist in the temple. He will *"opposeth and exalteth himself above all that is called God, or that is worshipped; so that he as God sitteth in the temple of God, shewing himself that he is God."* (See also Daniel 11:36.)

    (3) The Beast and the False Prophet begin their operation at mid-Tribulation (Revelation 13:5, 11).

    (4) The mark of the Beast (666) is introduced at mid-Tribulation (Revelation 13:5, 18; 14:9).

    (5) The remnant of Israel is taken into hiding at mid-Tribulation (Revelation 12:6).

    (6) The converts of the 144,000 are raptured into heaven at mid-Tribulation (Revelation 7:9-17).

    (7) Angels preach the Gospel at mid-Tribulation (Revelation 14:6-7).

    (8) Revelation 11 depicts the ministry of the Two Witnesses that begin their ministry at mid-Tribulation and continues throughout the last half of the Tribulation. They are divinely protected until the final 3 ¹/₂ days of the Tribulation Period, then put to death. The Two Witnesses are resurrected on the final day of the Tribulation Period.

10. Daniel chapter 10.

    A. Daniel prays and fasts for three weeks.

    B. The archangel of war, Michael, comes on the *"first day . . . for thy words."*

    C. Daniel is told that Greece shall follow the Persian Empire (Daniel 10:20).

Notes: _____

_____

_____

_____

_____

_____

_____

_____

_____

_____

_____

11. Daniel chapter 11.

   A. The kings of the north describe *Assyria*.

   B. The kings of the south describe *Egypt*.

   C. Verses 36-37 identify the Antichrist as one that has no regard for *"the God of his fathers, nor the desire of women, nor regard any god: for he shall magnify himself above all."* The Antichrist will live a homosexual lifestyle as confirmed by Revelation 11:8 and Genesis 19.

12. Daniel chapter 12 – Beginning of Israel's Restoration.

   A. Verse 1 describes the archangel Michael intervening for Israel during *"a time of trouble, such as never was since there was a nation."* This refers to the Holocaust.

   B. Restoration.

   C. Harvest (verse 3).

      (1) The Wise (Proverbs 11:30).

   D. Insight to the *"time of the end"* (verse 4), or the "last days."

      (1) Many shall run to and fro (great mobility of man).

      (2) Knowledge shall be increased.

         a. Acts 2:17 describes the "last days" with the outpouring of the Holy Spirit on the day of Pentecost.

         b. Joel 2:28 describes the "last days" after the restoration of Israel (the Fig Tree[6] – Joel 2:22), and continues throughout the Tribulation (Joel 2:31 and Matthew 24:29).

         c. II Timothy chapter 3 describes the "last days" as:

            (i) Perilous times shall come.

            (ii) Men shall be lovers of their own selves.

            (iii) Without natural affection.

            (iv) Lovers of pleasures more then lovers of God.

            (v) Ever learning, and never able to come to the knowledge of the truth.

-----

[6]The Fig Tree is a biblical type of Israel (Jeremiah 24; Hosea 9:10).

d. Hebrews 1:1-2 describes the "last days" as a time when God would speak to us by His Son. He has been doing so for over 2,000 years.

e. Jude 18 describes this period as the *"last time"* when *"there should be mockers . . . who should walk after their own ungodly lusts."*

E. The rebirth of Israel (Daniel 12:11-12).

(1) The site of the daily sacrifice began with the offering of Isaac on Mount Moriah (Genesis 22).

(2) Mount Moriah became the place in the temple of Jerusalem where the sacrifices were offered.

(3) Mount Moriah is the same place where followers of Islam believe Mohammed ascended into heaven at the time of his death in *632 A.D.*

(4) As a result, the Israeli place of sacrifice was replaced by the Islamic Dome of the Rock.

(5) The year 632 A.D., plus 1290 years, equals the year 1922 – the year Churchill implemented the pending Balfour Declaration, the British mandate that provided a homeland for Israel in Palestine.

(6) The year 632 A.D., plus 1335 years, equals 1967 – the year Israel recaptured the city of Jerusalem (June 7, 1967). The *"times of the Gentiles"* began when Jerusalem fell into Babylonian captivity as recorded in Daniel chapter 1 (approximately 605-586 B.C.). The process of prophetic fulfillment continues through June 7, 1967 (Luke 21:24). That prophecy is completed at the conclusion of the Tribulation (Revelation 11:1-2). As the *"blindness"* of Israel is removed at that time, all of Israel is saved (Romans 11:25).

(7) June 7, 1967 marked the first time that Jerusalem was under Israeli rule since the city was captured and burned by King Nebuchadnezzar in 586 B.C.

Notes: _____ __

_____

_____

_____

_____

_____

_____

_____

Study in the Book of Daniel

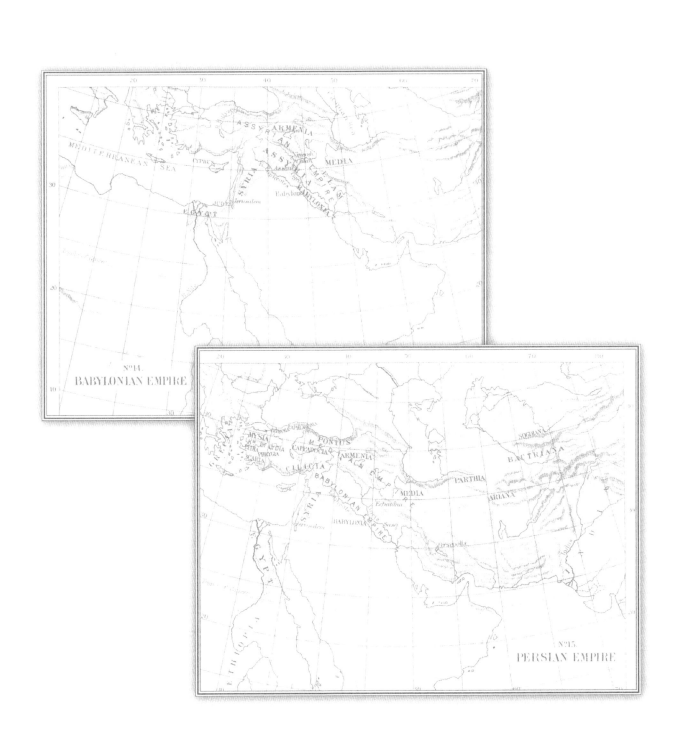

Nº14.
BABYLONIAN EMPIRE

Nº15.
PERSIAN EMPIRE

Charts and Maps

Kingdom of Israel Divided (931 B.C.)

Fall of the Northern Kingdom - Israel to Assyria (721-713 B.C.)

Judah	**Israel**	**Nineveh**	**Edom**
Joel (830-750 B.C.)	Amos (760-753 B.C.)	Jonah (782-753 B.C.)	Obadiah (840 B.C.)
Isaiah (740-680 B.C.)	Hosea (760-720 B.C.)	Nahum (663-612 B.C.)	
Micah (735-710 B.C.)			

Fall of the Southern Kingdom - Judah to Babylon 608-605 B.C.*

Judah	**Babylon**	
Zephaniah (640-609 B.C.)	Daniel (605-530 B.C.)	
	King's Court	
		* Siege I (608-605 B.C.)
Habakkuk (606 B.C.)	Ezekiel (593-571 B.C.)	Siege II (597 B.C.)
	Babylonian Captivity	Siege III (588-586 B.C.)
Jeremiah (626-586 B.C.)		Jerusalem Destroyed

Restoration of Jerusalem and the Temple (Persia 539-425 B.C.)

Jerusalem

Haggai (520 B.C.)	Zechariah (520-518 B.C. & 480-470 B.C.)	Malachi (432-425 B.C.)

First return from Persia		**Second return from Persia**	**Third return from Persia**
Zerubbabel (536-515 B.C.)	Esther (483-473 B.C.)	Ezra (457 B.C.)	Nehemiah (444-425 B.C.)
Rebuilds the Temple.	*Queen of Persia.*	*Restores the people.*	*Rebuilds the walls and city.*

Study in the Book of Daniel

The Seventy Weeks of Daniel

Daniel 9:24-27

Sixty-Nine Weeks = 483 Years

444 B.C.   33 A.D.

[_____]

The decree of Persian King Artaxerxes I   The Messiah "Cut Off"
to Rebuild Jerusalem   (Daniel 9:25)
(Nehemiah 2:1-8 / Daniel 9:25)

Daniel's 70th Week
The Tribulation – Jacob's Trouble*

One Week = 7 Years

3 $^1/_2$ Years   3 $^1/_2$ Years
(42 months = 1260 days)   (42 months = 1260 days)

[_____[_____]

First half of the Tribulation   *Second half of the Tribulation

Note: Prophetic Year = 12 months of 30 days each / 360 days annually.

The 7,000 Years of Man

Adam to Abraham	**Abraham to Jesus**	**Church Age**	**Millennium**
2,000 Years	2,000 Years*	2,000 Years	1,000 Years

[_____[_____[_____] 7 Years [_____] **Eternity**

800 Years
400 Years | 400 Years   **The Tribulation**
O.T. Prophets   God's Silence

* Includes seven-year Tribulation Period.

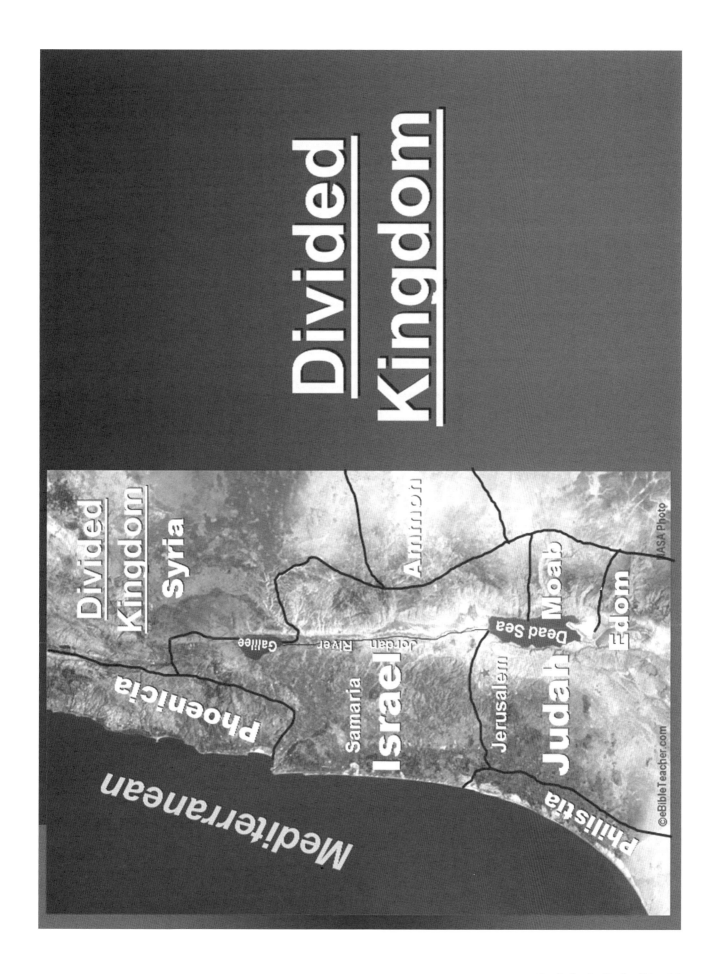

Study in the Book of Daniel

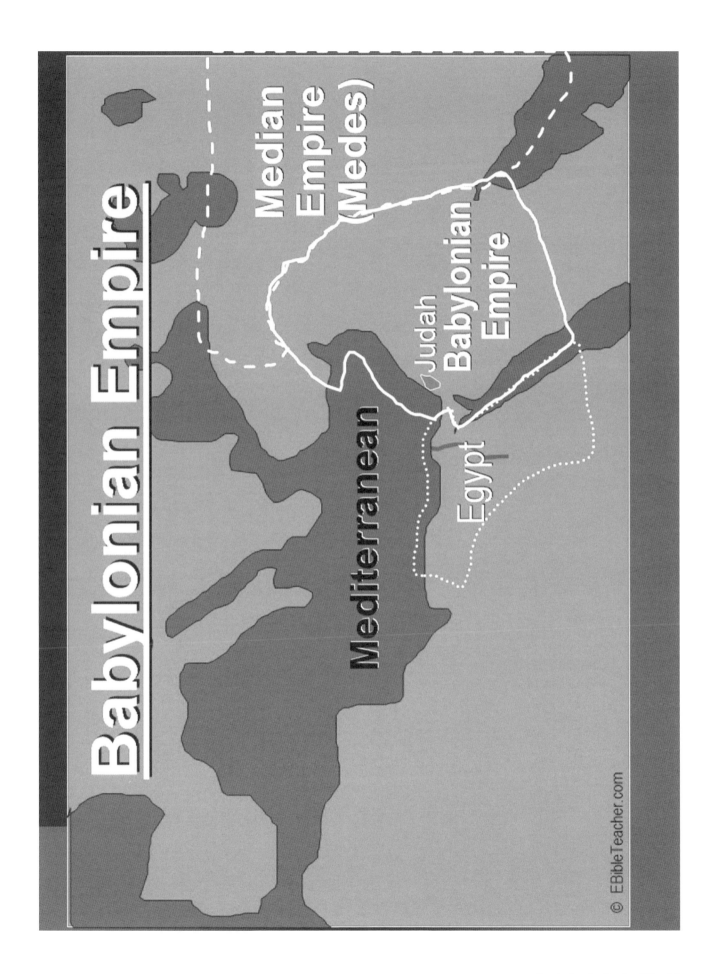

Study in the Book of Daniel

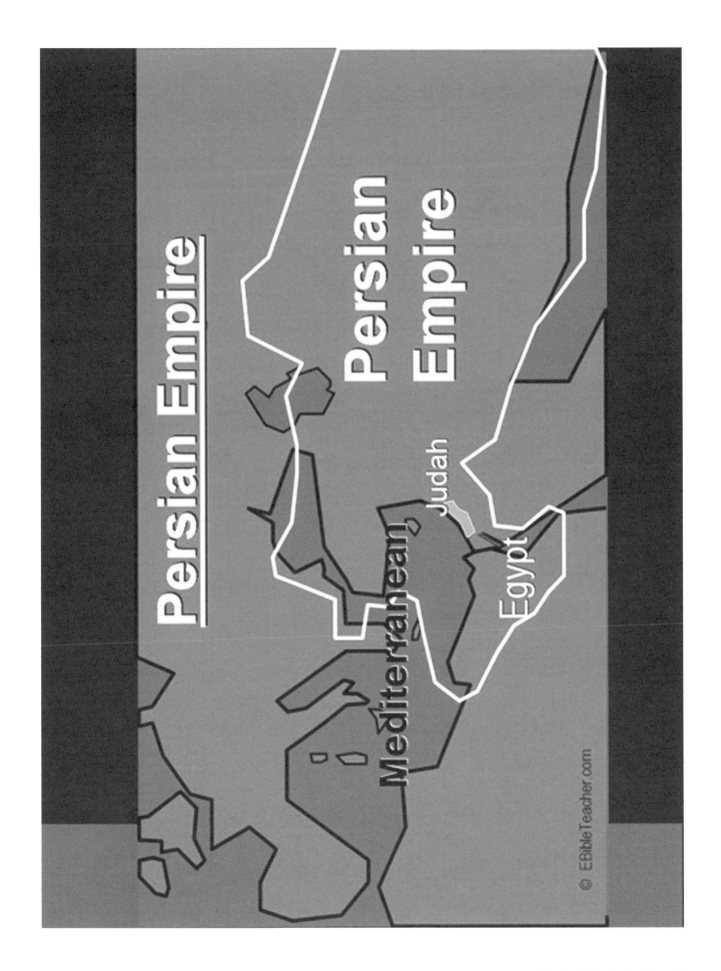

45

Study in the Book of Daniel